a visual panorama of London's
country buses and bus operations
over the years

a Lo
Cou

GW01044819

from Broadway to Bell Street

compiled by
Ray Stenning &
Trevor Whelan

with photographic contributions from others

design by Ray Stenning/Viewfinder

photoset in 7pt and 8pt Univers
printed on Stargloss Art 115 gsm
by Acanthus Press, Wellington, Somerset

bound by
W. H. Ware & Sons Ltd., Clevedon, Avon

24 Silver Street
Wiveliscombe
Somerset TA4 2PB

ISBN 0 906051 01 0

London's green

A London Country Bus seems a contradiction of terms, for one doesn't usually associate London with the country. But when the London Passenger Transport Board was formed in 1933 to control London's bus services its operations included many that were of a decidedly rural nature. Routes that had been operated by East Surrey in the south and by National in the north, together with the Green Line network of limited stop links to Town and beyond, were the basis of the 'green' bus area. These had briefly formed London General Country Services in 1932. The area extended around the capital from Horsham to Hitchin, from Guildford to Grays, and from Amersham to Sevenoaks. Some services ran outside the designated area — beyond Hildenborough to Tonbridge and Tunbridge Wells, and beyond East Grinstead to Forest Row, for example.

Through four decades London Transport served London's green. Green Line carried people to the capital or into the country, green buses took shoppers from village to town, between towns, to wherever they ran. The buses themselves were the same handsome London designs, only green. The single-deck fleet was more specialised than the double-deck before the war but even Green Line Ts, underfloor-engined TFs and side-engined Qs were unmistakably 'London' buses. Little one-man Cubs were virtually the same red or green. In post-war years standardisation reached its near monotonous peak. Only the Cubs' replacement GS class and non-standard lowbridge RLHs added variety to a basically two class fleet — double-deck RT and single-deck RF, the latter in both bus and coach versions almost identical!

In 1970 big upheavals in passenger transport following the 1968 Transport Act brought a new company to operate the 'green buses', London Country Bus Services Ltd. It seemed much as before in its first year of existence but before long the split from London Transport began to be apparent. Familiar LT trappings disappeared and, after a temporary revised livery and 'flying polo' logo, the all-embracing National Bus Company identity soon took hold.

Priority was given to LCBS by NBC administration to renew its ageing fleet. Twenty-year-old RTs and RFs were still in a majority. Soon new types were arriving in great variety but maintenance problems bedevilled the first few years, keeping many older vehicles on borrowed time. By 1977 the LT connection was still evident in several ways but London Country was now unmistakably a National bus company.

A touch of history repeating itself occurred as the company's headquarters were established at Bell Street, Reigate, formerly headquarters of the East Surrey empire.

Adjustments in border areas, involving the transfer of services to and from neighbouring NBC companies in the interests of operating economy, and to some long-established route patterns, especially the Green Line system, together with the inevitable withdrawal of certain routes — often through cessation of local authority grants — were made to meet changing travel needs.

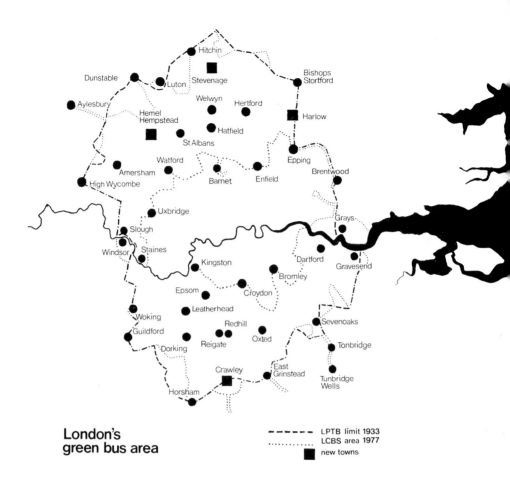

Hitchin

Dunstable   Luton   Stevenage   Bishops Stortford

Aylesbury   Welwyn   Hertford

Hemel Hempstead   Harlow

Hatfield

St Albans   Epping

Watford   Brentwood

Amersham   Barnet   Enfield

High Wycombe

Uxbridge

Slough   Grays

Windsor   Staines

Kingston   Dartford

Bromley   Gravesend

Epsom   Croydon

Woking   Leatherhead

Redhill   Sevenoaks

Guildford

Dorking   Reigate   Oxted   Tonbridge

Crawley   East Grinstead

Horsham   Tunbridge Wells

London's green bus area

- – – – – – LPTB limit 1933
.... LCBS area 1977
■ new towns

But what has remained constant is the attraction of the area. Hill ranges sweep across the southern part to include such famous landmarks as Leith Hill, highest point in south-east England, and Box Hill, and interesting houses like Winston Churchill's Chartwell, near Westerham. The Chilterns form an arc along the north-west fringes, though the green buses of London have reached out beyond the steep scarp slope to the Buckinghamshire town of Aylesbury. Luton Hoo and Knebworth House lie in the northern part, while literary connections are maintained by Milton's cottage and the churchyard famed by Thomas Gray, both at Chalfont St. Giles.

Old towns like St. Albans or Dorking and designated new towns of Crawley, Hemel Hempstead, Stevenage and Harlow combine with pretty villages, wild commons and green woods to form the background to our visual panorama of London's country buses and bus operations — our London Country Bus album.

It would be impossible to show every aspect that we would wish, and no doubt you will find some things missing. We have been biased by our own feelings and, although it is a personal selection, nevertheless we have compiled a staggering array of observations, of facts and comments, enriched by the dedicated camerawork of many famous London bus photographers (all mentioned at the end) that together capture the unique flavour of the London Country Bus scene.

It is not intended as a history — thought there is much to learn from the following pages — it is, rather, a compilation of events and scenes, of times and places; of things familiar and unusual, old and new; of the overlooked and the things you never thought to look at — there are things we never thought to look at before! But here in pictures, words, maps and diagrams, is our selection, our **London Country Bus album** . . .

No account of London's country buses or bus services would be complete without mention of the RT. Perhaps the ultimate in standardisation, the RT double-decker could almost be described as The London Bus of all time! From the withdrawal of the last green STL (the RT's predecessor) in 1955 until the introduction of Routemasters to the Country Area in 1965, it was the sole double-decker type in Country bus service. For several years Tunbridge Wells (TW) alone was without an RT allocation (it only worked the 704), and Grays (GY) for a time was nothing but RT.

Such standardisation brought monotony to the Country Bus network during that time, and even at the takeover by London Country in 1970 there were more than 450 RTs still in everyday revenue earning service. Leatherhead (LH), for example, had 42 RTs for its M-F scheduled double-deck vehicle requirements.

Nose to nose at Harlow (HA), RT 964 and RT 4550 elegantly pass the time of day.

Chelsham (CM) once supplied RTs for the 403 group, local 453 and the 408/470 routes. This latter pair were shared with LH (both) and GF (408). Seen at CM in 1966 is RT 4727 from GF before returning on its long journey via Croydon to Guildford. Behind it RT 4754 leaves on a 403 with another RT approaching. CM was still operating RTs in the summer of 1977.

the Chelsham RT

RTs in south east service

Following the verdant Darent valley useful 401 from Belvedere & Dartford to Sevenoaks was an RT stronghold. Further RTs could be found on routes at each end of its journey. At Dartford it met the busy 480 from Erith to Gravesend, RML operated from 1966. RT 2754 (NF) at Market Street in the last year of RT operation *(upper left)*.

Sevenoaks later became predominantly a single-deck area but in 1965 RTs were still in abundance. RT 1088 (DG) in the bus station on local route to Heverham *(lower left)*. In the first days of 1972 it was diverted instead to Noahs Ark, replacing part of M&D 55.

RTs on East Grinstead locals

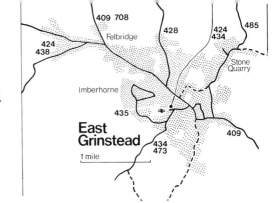

The operations of Sargent's of East Grinstead were acquired by Southdown bit by bit from 1933 to 1951. However, their workers' services to Crawley and Gatwick were passed on to London Transport in April 1951, who formed them into the 438/A, later to include B & C suffix variations too.

RT 2741 (EG) shows a double-blind display for the 438C on a schoolday working near Felbridge *(top)*. The 438 family has always had an irregular timetable supplementing parallel routes during rush hours. When the Three Bridges-Tunbridge Wells branch line closed at the start of 1967 extra 438A journeys were provided, but eventually all were rationalised to become plain 438.

Despite some residents' protests, town route 435 to the Imberhorne Estate started on the 9th December 1964. It then had a flat fare of 4d (old money!) and was worked by crew RTs, crew & OMO RFs. In 1973 it was diverted to travel via the Gardenwood development, as shown on the 1977 East Grinstead bus map above. When still taking the direct route to the estate, RT 3218 (EG) passes the bus garage on its return to the town in 1966 *(lower)*.

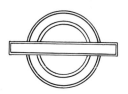

Green Line RTs from Aldgate

Some RTs were built as Green Line vehicles for the busy East London routes from Aldgate into south Essex, though the difference from bus versions was minimal. Allocated to Romford (RE) and Grays (GY), their numbers swelled when 28 more were converted to this dubious status in 1960. The original 'coaches' sported a bullseye motif in relief on the between-decks panel, whereas the later versions bore simple transfers, and internally all were identical to ordinary buses — even having open platforms!

The original network became quite extensive, involving 721/2/3 and suffix variations, but by autumn 1977 the 723 to Grays was the sole survivor, RTs having long since vanished from the routes.

The 722 was extended from its Upminster, Corbets Tey terminus in November 1963 through Dartford tunnel to Dartford, but cut back after a year.

RT 4509 (GY) in 1964 at East Ham en route to Grays *(above)*. Then the 723A went via Belhus and the 723 via Stonehouse Corner. The raised motif can be clearly seen.

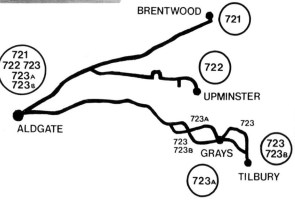

As RCLs were introduced to take their place they became dispersed to other garages for bus duties or sold, but quite a number had already been at other garages for Green Line reliefs often appearing on bus routes. RT 605 (GR), of the later type with 'tween-decks transfers, at Uxbridge in October 1964 on the 347 *(below)*.

RTs forlorn & reborn

A cold March day in 1976 caught RT 4783 at the back of Grays garage — battered and dented, without blinds, headlights or even engine (left). In the hard times of the early seventies when parts were in short supply, many buses were cannibalised to keep others on the road.

Many RTs were still giving good service however, some a quarter of a century after they first took the road. By 1st May 1977 London Country's contingent of the once numerous class had dwindled to 22 but a handful of these venerable vehicles were recertified and outshopped from Tinsley Green Works resplendent in full NBC colours, perhaps the best livery they had ever worn. They went to CM for the 403, RT 1018 first. RT 604 had the distinction of being (after Southern Vectis's open-top Bristol K5G) the oldest bus in the entire NBC, and is seen leaving Chelsham garage bus park (below). The 403 had a variety of vehicles at that time — notice also the hired Maidstone Atlantean among RMC & RCL types.

ROUTEMASTER ROUTES

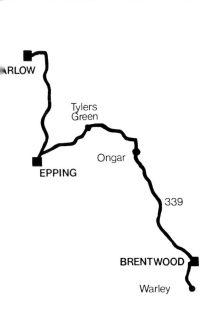

RLOW

Tylers Green

Ongar

EPPING

339

BRENTWOOD

Warley

Route 339 links Harlow New Town with Brentwood continuing to the Ford works at Warley, serving Epping and Ongar on the way. Despite using busy A-roads for most of its length it serves a quite rural area and often carries light loads. In July 1977 it went over to complete single-deck OMO operation, the Sunday service being s/d OMO for some time (see page 26). Three weeks before the conversion RML 2352 (HA) was caught in scenery typical of that route (below). RT 621 (HA) on a 339 short to Ongar seen in Harlow in 1975 (opposite) offers comparison between RT and Routemaster.

Of integral construction, initially intended for London trolleybus replacement, the Routemaster was hailed as London's Bus of the Future — this slogan was actually emblazened on the side advert panels on the prototypes. The basic design dates from the early fifties (RM 1 appeared in 1954), so that by the time Country Area examples were placed in service a decade had passed and the concept of a traditional front-engined, rear open platform double-decker was being questioned.

However, having made its mark in the Central Area and been introduced to selected Green Line routes the Routemaster, in its 30' long 72-seat bus guise classified RML, entered green Country service on 3rd October 1965 to routes 409/10/1 (see page 76). RM 2, the second prototype, had in fact seen brief service in green livery for a few months in 1957 on the 406 Redhill-Kingston route.

Altogether 100 of these 72-seaters were delivered in 1965/6 in two batches separated by further red examples: 2306-2355 (CUV 306-355C) and 2411-2460 (JJD 411-460D). The green RMLs had semi-automatic 4-speed gearboxes rather than the fully automatic of the red ones, to suit their different operating conditions.

They were introduced on to selected busy trunk routes, sometimes with a slight lessening in service frequency. Route 480, seen under RT charge on page 6, went over to RML in November 1965. Still operated by the handsome type a dozen years later, RML 2342 (NF) of the first batch is seen at Dartford *(top left)*. Other routes got RMLs in 1966, including the 306/311/347/484 & 805. Windsor's National-liveried RML 2357 of the second batch is seen here at Slough Bus Station in April 1977 on the 441 from High Wycombe to Staines *(lower left)*. The AEC/LT radiator badge has been removed under London Country ownership on both vehicles.

In late 1969, just prior to the formation of LCBS, three green RMLs (2321/2441/3) were exchanged with three red XA Atlanteans, needed to replace XFs sent from EG to SV for the Blue Arrow experimental service. Thus London Country took over a fleet of 97 RMLs — supplemented by 69 RMCs and 43 RCLs — of LT designed Routemasters.

These RMC and RCL coach versions of the Routemaster were again brave hopes for the future. CRL 4 was delivered in 1957 as the last of four prototype Routemasters, redesignated RMC 4 in 1961. The 68 production RMCs, 1453-1520, entered service on Green Line routes 715/A, 716/A, 718, 719, 720/A during 1962, followed in 1965 by the longer 65-seat RCLs numbered 2218-2260, allocated first to the famous Aldgate routes.

Their life on Green Line work was short. In early 1969 some RMCs were demoted to bus work from HF & WY on the 303/A & 461A and by 1972 only three Routemasters were still performing regular coach duties, these at GD for the RCL operated rush hour 709. As new single-decker coaches were delivered RMC/RCL vehicles rapidly became familiar as bus types on such routes as 405, 414, the 330/A and the 370. February 1972 saw RMCs at DT for the 499. RMC 1480 in Hythe Street, Dartford, in June 1977 *(below)*. The differing destination screen of the coach version can be clearly seen. RMC 4 always had the standard bus Routemaster layout *(see page 69)*.

ORPINGTON

477

Two months after the 499 conversion, RMCs displaced from GF by new RPs went to Swanley (SJ) for the 477 Dartford-Chelsfield route. RMCs were no strangers to SJ as it had operated them earlier on Green Line 717. This view of RMC 1492 in Orpington *(above)* shows the messy rear-end styling necessitated by incorporating an emergency exit due to folding platform doors. RMC 1484 was the first to receive National livery in July 1973, a livery better suited to the Routemaster lines than any other they have worn.

RCL 2237 (GD) outside its home garage on the rush-hours only 709 when the type could still be found on other Green Line routes *(lower left)*. Shiny RCL 2220 (RE) in early 1966 at Aldgate *(lower right)*. Green Line Routemasters initially had the traditional pale green painted raised window surrounds. A later livery modification had them painted over in the main body colour.

sting
in
the
tail

Country buses with engines at the back

Widespread elsewhere since the late '50s, rear-engined double-deckers didn't arrive in quantity to London's country until the early '70s. But they weren't a totally new concept to Country Bus operation.

In 1965, when LT were investigating various new vehicles, a batch of 50 standard Leyland Atlantean/Park Royal double-deckers arrived for the Central Area (XA) and eight identically bodied Daimler Fleetlines for the Country Area (XF). They were to be swopped around for comparison purposes (together with RMLs in the Central Area) to find the most suitable bus for future London service. Another part of the experiment was to use the Fleetlines one-man in the off-peak, with the top deck chained out of use — neither the MoT nor the unions would permit one-man double-deckers at the time.

With its Leyland 0.680 engine working hard at the back, AN 71 (CY) freshly painted in NBC colours, climbs into view on Crawley local 479.

The eight Fleetlines entered service on September 15th 1965 from EG on the cross-country 424 between Reigate & East Grinstead. It was considered an ideal route for the experiment, having slack periods between heavy peaks. XF 6, before any trials started, stopping in East Grinstead High Street the following March shows the original liver *(above)*.

Apart from a temporary brief exchange with red Atlanteans as part of the comparison tests early on and the absence of XF 6-8 for Blue Arrow work at SV between 1969 and 1972, all have remained in use at EG. Operating schedules have brought them to other EG routes — 428 *(see page 86)*, 435 and peak-hours-only 438. XF 1 returns through the Gardenwood Estate on the 435 in July 1977 *(left)*. Look at the map on page 7. That magnificent viaduct once carried trains on their way from London through incomparable Sussex countryside along what in 1960 became the famous Bluebell line.

The distinctive but plain rear end of the earlier back-engined buses is shown by NBC-liveried XF 3 leaving Crawley on a schoolday 438 *(lower left)*. From 1966 to 1973 this particular bus had its usual Gardner 6LX engine replaced by a Cummins V6, with structural alterations to the 'bustle' to accommodate it.

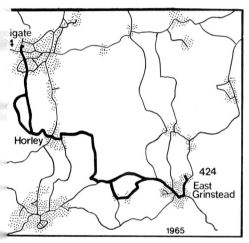

424

East Grinstead

1965

Three red XAs were drafted in to EG in late 1969 to allow XF 6-8 to take up their Stevenage Blue Arrow work. Painted green with yellow relief and the new logo in May 1970, XA 46-48 were among the first London Country vehicles to appear in the new livery. When LT sold their XAs to Hong Kong in 1973 these three went too, and in replacement three more of the AN class mentioned below were ordered. Built to standard NBC specification they were allocated to EG alongside the XFs. New AN 122 speeds past The Abergavenny Arms near Copthorne shortly after delivery in 1974 *(above)*. The different staircase position of its Park Royal body can be clearly seen when compared with earlier ANs.

Another comparison is offered between one of this batch and XF 1 outside EG garage *(below)*. The increase in window size is most noticeable.

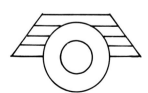

However, the first new double-deck arrivals for London Country were 11 Leyland-engined Fleetlines with N Counties two-door bodies, a diverted order from Western Welsh. These AFs entered service in February 1972 from GD on the famous 410 *(see page 80)*. AF 1 at Bromley North Station in the new light green/yellow they introduced to London Country *(opposite top)*.

Following delivery of AFs came the ANs, similar two-door buses for busy trunk routes. The first 90 were actually a London Country order but the other 30, like the AFs above, were a diverted order, only from Midland Red. Park Royal built the bodywork on AN 1-90, MCW on 91-120. Subtle detail differences, such as lower front panels and screen, can be seen on AN 18 (Park Royal) and AN 105 (MCW), both from LS on the long and busy, equally famous 321 from Uxbridge to Luton *(above)*.

Common enough in most other NBC fleets, the Bristol VR/ECW combination made its London Country debut in 1977 when 15 of the type entered service at Grays, bringing complete double-deck one-man-operation a step nearer realisation. BT 6 (GY) on the 368 to the Bata shoe factory *(opposite lower)*.

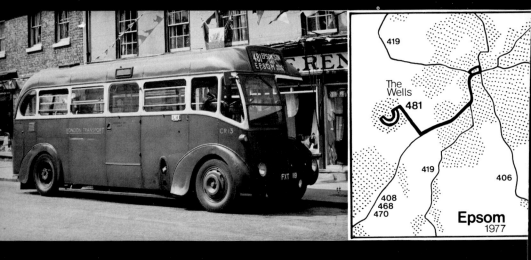

The generation of rear-engined single-deckers spawned by rather inadequate trials of the mid-sixties were not the first to operate around the metropolis with power from behind.

Indeed, one has to go back nearly thirty years before that to the CR class of 1939. These were Leyland Cubs, but with the engine placed transversely at the rear, fortelling double-deck configuration of twenty years later, and fitted with modern, unmistakably LPTB-built bodywork. Actually red buses, several appeared after the war on Country routes, a few being repainted green in 1952 —withdrawn a year later.

CR 13 (LH) on route *(above)* and CR 33 (LH) at Epsom Station *(below)* on Epsom local 481, one time the Country Area's shortest route.

MBS 4 (CY), seen leaving Crawley's half-built Bewbush Estate, predates the bulk of the MB/MBS Merlin class by a couple of years but didn't actually enter London Country stock until 1973.

In 1966 six experimental Merlins with Strachans multi-standing two-door bodywork entered LT service on Red Arrow 500. So successful was the service that eight of the nine similar, but conventionally seated XMBs intended for the Country Area were quickly converted to Red Arrows too.

The solitary Country bus XMB 1, later renumbered XMB 15 (later reclassified MBS), eventually entered service from RG in August 1967 registered SMM 15F — previous registrations allotted were JLA 57D & NHX 15E. After subsequent brief work at GR she went to TG for the 387 in 1969 and there remained until 1973, when she was returned to LT in exchange for MBS 4.

The rest of the Merlins had MCW bodywork of a less plain appearance — MB 81-113, B45D & MBS 270-303/398-438, B33 + 27D — and were delivered in 1968/9, the first to RG. Some were used for various Autofare experiments early on but most succumbed to conventional OMO.

MBS 438 (CY) visibly demonstrates its long low look at Langley Green *(above)*. CY was a mixture of MBS & SM for à long while but its last SMs were displaced by Merlins in 1976. MBS 406 (CY) passing through East Grinstead near the end of its shortened 434 journey in 1977 *(below)*.

SM 536 (WR) leaves behind The Packhorse at Gerrards Cross *(see page 85)* on the circuitous 335 route from Watford via The Chalfonts to Windsor *(above)*. In 1977 this bus still carried the original livery and logo.

AEC Swift
SM

The SM class of AEC Swifts, shorter versions of the Merlin, were ordered by London Transport prior to the 1970 split and were therefore numbered in the same series as LTs. However, the two batches received Surrey registrations — 101-148, BPH 101-148H & 449-538, DPD 449-538J. Park Royal bodied the first batch and Metro-Cammell the second, to the same basic pattern but with slightly different seating capacities. Interesting to observe that although shorter than the Merlins, they had 6-bay window construction in place of the 5½-bay of the longer buses!

Showing NBC livery, SM 453 (MA), on hire to WR, picks up at Uxbridge Station working the 452 to Windsor *(right)*.

23

Swifts
from
SOUTH WALES

SMW SMA

London Country has strong connections with Sout
Transport. In 1971, when new vehicles were desper
not forthcoming, three long Swifts with 2-door BE
bodywork of 1969 vintage were bought from SWT
service at Crawley (CY), where extra buses were n
acquired from Southdown *(see pages 44 and 50)*.

SMW 1 (CY) heads out of Crawley through woode
near Ifield on circular 426 via Charlwood and Horle
route was not ex-Southdown.

A further 12 Swifts with
modern BET style single-
were also purchased from
these having been in serv
matter of weeks before l
them to their SMW class
service in the St Albans
1971.

SMW 11 (SA), in origina
St Albans in October 197
from Dunstable *(left).*

Their appearance was cl
considerably on overhau
also on the 343 but in 19
only NBC livery but also
rather fussy side and fro
embellishments, even th
(right).

Then in 1972 the SMA class entered Green Line service on south orbital 725. These 21 Swifts had 36' 1'' Alexander bodywork of an attractive appearance — from the inside too, with ramped floor and deep panoramic side windows for superb vision. Ordered by SWT as buses, they were diverted to London Country, who were in time to arrange for them to be equipped to coach specification instead.

SMA 20 was allocated to CY for a long while, being a suitable vehicle for excursions from that town. However, she was more often found on the 478 Broadfield route *(see page 44),* as shown here in June 1975 wearing pre-NBC livery *(above).*

eded but
tion style
tered
routes

yside
. This

t more
ywork
Wales,
a
ed
tered
in

rives at
343

(SA),
not
f the

ge

With its distinctive roof-mounted ventilation pod, the versatile Leyland National soon became a familiar sight on London Country routes following introduction of the first at the end of 1972. Of the 23 two-door 11 metre (37' 2'') versions classified LN, 1-4 received Superbus livery and the rest unrelieved leaf green, like LN 15 (HF) on Welwyn Garden City town route 848 *(below)*.

In February 1973 the first Green Line versions appeared, classified LNC, but their austere bus interiors were a retrograde step. Delivered in bus colours because of Leyland's inability to paint them in anything but all green or all red, London Country had to add the white above the waistline themselves (NBC 'local coach' livery). This was to be the new Green Line colour scheme. Later they were thankfully demoted to bus status *(see page 74)*.

NATIONAL
power

26

The following September the first short Nationals arrived. Classified SN at first, they entered Green Line service reclassified SNC. 71-115 still had 'un-Green Line like' interiors but deliveries from 116 were fitted with high-backed coach seating and inside roof luggage racks, enabling the earlier SNCs to be quickly downgraded to SNB bus status and assume bus duties replacing older vehicles. The first 'suburban coach' SNCs went to the 723. SNB 76 (HG), ex-SNC with 'bus' interior, was back on Green Line work temporarily when seen at Golders Green on the 716 to Hitchin *(top left)*. You can see how they perpetuated Green Line colours but without fleetnames in this role.

Many Nationals were delivered unlettered as well as unrelieved. SNB 266 shows this condition when new at Epping Station on a Sunday 339 OMO working before the route became completely OMO *(top right)*.

Phase 2 Nationals, with detail improvements, began to arrive in July 1976. SNB 248, near Dunton Green, shows the well-known rear profile and the white waist stripe, a livery modification found on all later NBC bus Nationals *(lower right)*.

London's little buses

One of London's best-loved Country bus types was the GS of 1953. On a Guy Special chassis, based on the Vixen, these 84 OMO buses were unique to the Country Area and could be found throughout the system, working from 16 garages in their heyday.

Many a young enthusiast must have puzzled over the 'FEATHERS IN OUR CAP' Red Indian mascot up front, a Guy trademark *(top left)*. The front end pressing was made by Briggs and could be seen on contemporary Ford Thames lorries as well.

GS 42 (HH) astride a Hemel Hempstead road in 1963 demonstrates the smart ECW bodywork *(lower left)*.

RFs began to oust GSs in the early '60s and by 1967 only 15 were scheduled for regular service. In London Country's early days it was down to one — for the 336A Rickmansworth-Loudwater Village, usually outstationed at the driver's home each night. The route ceased after 30th March 1972 and thus GS operation finally ended in London's country.

20 years earlier the route was Cub operated, as were most GS routes. C 60, from the soon to be replaced Watford, Leavesden Road garage (WT), at Rickmansworth *(below)*.

Also ECW bodied and worthy successors to the GSs, London Country's small buses on the Bristol LHS chassis (BL & BN) were really RF replacements where larger buses would be inappropriate or too unwieldy. The first of the 23 BLs arrived in June 1973, not entering service until October (at SA & DG) because of training difficulties with manual gearboxes. The last of this batch were allocated to Amersham (MA), such as BL 19, seen in Chesham soon after delivery in early 1974 *(middle right)*.

Later in 1974 the first of the narrower BNs arrived, numbered in the same series since their sole difference was in body width, only 7' 6''. BN 36 (HG) takes a 331 short working through Ware in 1975 *(lower right)*. The narrower ECW body has a neater sidelamp/indicator arrangement. Compare also the difference in bodyside overhang, being on the same chassis.

GS 55 (NF) on the 489A, a route detailed on page 52 *(top right)*. The GSs were fitted with Perkins P6 engines and crash gearboxes — pre-selective were standard on all other London buses at the time.

The first 20 of London's post-war lowbridge class, conventional AEC Regents with Weymann bodies, classified RLH, arrived in the summer of 1950. A diverted order from Midland General, they were supplemented in late 1952 by a further 56 ordered by LT. Amersham received the first six for the 336 but it wasn't long before the traditional outposts of lowbridge bus operation had their allocation — Addlestone and Godstone — and also Guildford since after 1950 its operations to Woking were linked with those from Staines and Walton to Woking.

East Grinstead actually got four of the green RLHs (the last 24 were painted red for the Central Area) though it had no specific need for the type! RLH 43, seen here *(left)* at Dormansland Plough, a location featured on page 86, stayed at EG until February 1955.

CAUTION LOW ROOF !
London's famous   RLH

However, the honours for stability in allocation must go to RLH 14. It left Weymann's Addlestone works in June 1950 and remained at Addlestone garage (WY), just down the road, for the next 20 years! It is seen here *(below)* in Woking in 1967 on the 463 to Walton, which kept the old routing when its companion 436 to Staines was diverted through the vast LCC Sheerwater Estate in 1953.

RLH 44 (WY) leaving Guildford's Onslow Street Bus Station on the 436 in 1966 *(top right)*. She made the unofficial last RLH public journey in London Country service on 31st July 1970 — arriving at the depot eight minutes after RLH 35's official last run! After withdrawal she was converted into a mobile uniform stores.

Restricted forward vision and minimal headroom of the upstairs interior *(right)*. Alighting from an inside seat at any time was awkward, in rush hours it was a game of musical chairs combined with the cakewalk!

Route 420 (West Byfleet-Sheerwater-Woking) received an RLH in 1959. 21 (WY), the first of the LT ordered batch, by Woking Station with A&D buses behind *(below)*. The full RLH story can be found in Peter Gascoine's superb book on the subject.

STLs in Essex

Route 339 yet again! On a garage journey and basking in the warm June sunshine, STL 2562 (EP) at Ongar in 1949 *(above)*. Then the 339 operated between Warley & Coxtie Green or Ongar only, the Epping section of road usually covered by the 392.

In view of a watchful copper, the driver of STL 2699 (GY), the antipenultimate member of the class, hand-signals right with a 371A short working in 1952 *(below)*. This bus was one of 20 post-war Regent Mk IIs delivered in 1945/6, with provincial-style Weymann H56R bodywork similar to the RLHs. Initially allocated to WA & LS for the 321/351, some were later transferred to HG *(see page 40)* & GY.

Manufacturers were developing lightweight single-deck chassis at the same time as the last RFs were being delivered to the Country Area in 1953, and London Transport hired in that year three such vehicles for evaluation. The RF was based on the heavier Regal IV chassis, of course. All three were painted in Green Line colours and were based at RG for much of their trial period, performing both bus and coach duties as part of the experiment.

PTE 592, a Leyland owned Tiger Cub with Saunders-Roe body, saw brief service in the Central Area too, but is here on Country bus work from RG, on top of the North Downs at Woldingham Ridge (top).

NLP 635 was a Park Royal/AEC integral Monocoach, a model that never caught on much. Also on the 447, but at Reigate Red Cross (left), it later passed to the West Monmouthshire company.

The other member of the 1953 trio was a standard Bristol/ECW LS5G, PHW 918, actually owned by Bristol Tramways rather than the manufacturer. On reversion to their stock it became the first of their production LS fleet as 2828.

TWO EXPERIMENTAL TRIOS

The RW class of 1960 was bought by LT for evaluation of the 2-door concept for Country bus work. The three members of the class, standard AEC Reliance/ Willowbrook dual-doorway buses, operated from a variety of garages. RW 1 on the 427 while at WY (right).

All three were sold to Chesterfield Corporation in 1963. Note the unusual roof observation windows.

Old Reigate

London's green is richly endowed with interesting and historic towns, many of which were old market towns and first saw bus services at an early date. Reigate, with its market place in the centre, is particularly significant through being once the headquarters of Anthony Hawkins' East Surrey empire and now the headquarters of London Country. It always was effectively the main garage of the LT Country Area.

Reigate
& Redhill

POST-WAR

Outside Reigate garage and gleaming new in 1953, RF 521 (RG) is working the tortuous 447 road *(left)*. All RF routes were still crew-operated then. Town congestion and several steep hills made the route a suitable test for buses on trial, along with Green Line 711, also from RG. 447 Woldingham journeys involving the severe Caterham Hill descent (and climb) were later replaced by a 440 extension.

RF 521 was altered to Green Line specification and renumbered 302 in the 1956 shuffle within the class. In 1962 she reverted to a Country bus and the involved saga of her unique batch is told in **a London RF album.**

Side-engined Q types were a part of the Redhill/Reigate scene before the advent of RFs. Two examples, with their distinctive sloping roof BRCW bodies, do business at Redhill Market Place on the 447 *(lower left)*.

'Unfrozen' STL 2670 (RG) in Bell Street in 1952 on local 430 *(above)*.

'Godstone' STL 1055 (GD) adds a touch of brightness to a wet Reigate street *(below)*.

Leith Hill

DORKING

Dorking lies at the southern end of the Mole gap through the North Downs, on the busy A25 road. Famous nearby Boxhill and Leith Hill have made it a popular destination and public transport came early.

Map showing routes: Morden, Croydon, Epsom, Leatherhead, Guildford, Warlingham, Reigate, DORKING. Route numbers: 70, 470, 425.

Only six miles from Reigate, East Surrey first served Dorking in February 1914, a fortnight after Aldershot & District arrived from Guildford and three months before General came down from South London. Local concerns had unsuccessfully served the town as early as 1903.

LGOC route 70 (originally 107) later became joint with East Surrey and entered the LT era as a joint Central/Country route. In 1938 it became completely Country operated and diverted at Ewell to run to Warlingham (along the 408 road) instead of Morden. In 1966 RT 1020 (LH) was seen at Dorking bus garage terminus *(above)*.

Dorking garage (DS) wasn't built until 1932, most routes being worked from Reigate up to then.

In 1929 Skylark commenced a coach route from High Wycombe to Dorking via Reigate (the basis of the later 711) but withdrew in 1930 after Green Line started their more direct route to London from Dorking, lettered D in 1931. This was soon replaced by the K routes, one of which served Horsham, and after the war became 712/3/4 operated by TF coaches. TF 44 (SA) on 713 layover at Dorking *(below)*.

Coldharbour, the nearest point for Leith Hill, was reached in 1930 by East Surrey 33 from Dorking, and extended to Ranmore at the other end in 1934. Showing a numberless blind, C 3, on its way to Coldharbour in 1952, avoids a car in a high-banked narrow lane, one reason why larger buses were precluded *(opposite top)*. Picking up by the garage in May 1966 was GS 39 *(above)*. Coldharbour ceased to be served by London buses in 1968 but regained a summer Sundays circular 'Rambler's bus', county supported 417, in 1977.

In 1933 the previously joint with Aldershot & District Dorking-Guildford route became LT Country (only) 425. It was combined with the circular 439 in 1973 to provide a complex 425 Guildford-Dorking-Redhill/439 Guildford-Dorking-Newdigate-Dorking operation. Ex-Green Line RF 175 on a Guildford bound 425 from Redhill in 1977 *(below)*.

Like Reigate and Dorking, the market town of St Albans — or to be correct, the City of St Albans — first saw bus services at an early date, mostly provided by the Watford based National company. The city's twin attractions — the site of Verulamium, with its Roman theatre remains and wall, and the magnificent Norman abbey church — have made it a natural focus and bus and coach routes centre on the town. The broad, tree-lined main thoroughfare of St Peter's Street has the bus garage (built in 1936) conveniently at the northern end.

Whipsnade Zoo at the Country Area's edge, reached from St Albans in 1977 by Green Line express 737 or a 313 Enfield-St Albans extension (both summer only), was reached by the 368 in 1949, when STL 2069 (SA), one of a batch with corrosion-prone all-metal Park Royal bodywork, was caught in Green Line markings shifting the crowds intent on a day at the zoo *(above)*. Several STLs were so repainted at the start of the war when reduced 'bus' type Green Line services were introduced.

The busy Hertford-St Albans route started in 1921, developed to form the Hertford or South Hatfield to St Albans 341. RMC 1520 passes MBS 430 (SA) in St Peter's Street *(below)*. This Merlin is working route S4, one of the radial services cross-linking satellite areas of the town through the centre, revised and renumbered S1-6 in October 1976.

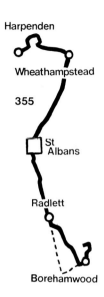

Harpenden

Wheathampstead

355

St Albans

Radlett

Borehamwood

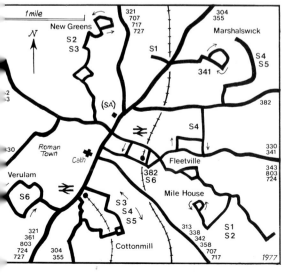

The 355 is a well-known single-deck Country route, linking St Albans with Radlett and Borehamwood. When Q 87 (SA) was photographed in St Albans in 1949 the route used the main A5 Watling Street between Radlett and Borehamwood (top). This was one of the several Country bus Qs converted for Green Line use — note the heater air intake and roof board brackets.

Some ten years later the 355 was extended northwards from St Albans to reach Harpenden via Wheathampstead, and ten years later still diverted at Radlett to take the direct road to Borehamwood.

The first of London Country's short Bristol LH buses had full width bodywork and were classified BL. (Subsequent BNs were only 7' 6'' wide.) BL 16 (SA) leaving for Borehamwood in 1975 (lower).

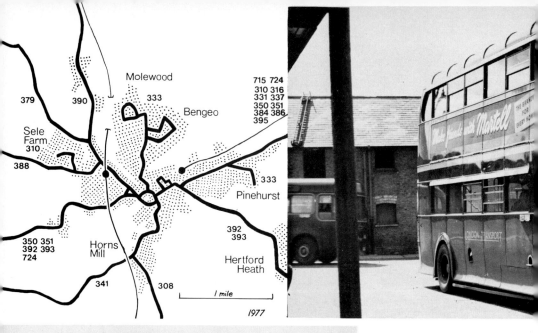

Map showing Hertford area routes (1977): Molewood, Bengeo, Pinehurst, Hertford Heath, Sele Farm, Horns Mill. Route numbers: 379, 390, 333, 715 724, 310 316, 331 337, 350 351, 384 386, 395, 310, 388, 333, 392 393, 350 351 392 393 724, 341, 308. Scale: 1 mile. 1977

For a County town, it's strange th
service didn't start until early 1921
began operating between Hertforc
was quite extensive when Nationa
September that year with their rou
LGOC also reached Hertford the s
relented in favour of the brown an
H&B routes passed to National in
independents was usually *laissez-*
Services and Biss Brothers also o
remaining independent until LPTB

In post-war livery, post-war STL 2
non-standard Weymann bodywor

Roof-box RT 971 in 1952. Hertforc
changed over the years but in 197
the 372 number, shown here by G
later to be found in the High Wyc

London's little buses on Hertford
nearer Cub, C 31, was in red livery
the since defunct Chapmore End

Route 327 in London Country day
destination display *(right)*. The 32
1977.

rd's first bus
arvey & Burrows
rmley. Their network
d on the scene in
St. Albans. The
briefly, but
buses of H&B! All
ose attitude to
ple's Motor
the area, the latter
n in 1933.

displays its

ave been much
still ran, though
TF 7 *(left),* was
a.

top right). The
GS 27 in 1963 at

604 with reduced
ent in January

THE
OLD TOWNS

Hertford

London's green since the war has hosted no fewer than four new towns, three in the northern area. The solution to a rising SE population, they have also bred problems of their own — coping with increased car use on local travel an example.

London Country, DoE and Stevenage Development Corporation have challenged this with a carefully monitored programme in local bus development. The Blue Arrow pre-booked home-to-work service began at the end of 1969. A pilot 809 graded-fare service pre-dated the start, on 31st July 1971, of SB1, a rapid high frequency flat-fare route from Chells to the town centre (and the industrial area during peaks), to promote bus as a better alternative to car for these journeys.

Public involvement through trials and questionnaires decided many things, even the distinctive yellow/blue livery and SB motif for Superbus, as it was to be known.

Further Superbus routes followed. LN 20 on SB3 from Martins Wood *(top)*. Occasionally ordinary buses deputise. AN 27 passing the resited station on SB2 *(middle)*.

Metro-Scanias featured in the trials, resulting in LC buying four and later exchanging three LNs for three Hants & Dorset ex-King Alfred Metro-Scanias, these seven the only examples in the NBC. In Stevenage bus station on SB1 is Hants-registered MS 6 with MS 1 *(below)*.

NEW TOWNS Success in the '70s

STEVENAGE

SB 2 · St Nicholas
Martins Wood
Chells
SB 3
SB 1

& failure

FT 5 (HA) on Harlow's 'PICK-ME-UP' service. Operated by LCBS for Harlow DC and the TRRL, using five Ford Transit/Dormobiles FT 1-5, this dial-a-ride for Old Harlow started on 31st August 1974 as another check on rising in-town car use.

Withdrawal of support ended the experiment in September 1976, being replaced by an off-peak fixed route. In April 1977 this was replaced by a midibus route to Old Harlow.

Crawley 1977

New Town and Old Town adjoin in natural harmony. Buses have always used the centre of the street by The George.

The only southern area
New Town, Crawley, is
unique among them in
having a garage built in
pre-LT days. Parked
outside, alongside
ubiquitous MBSs,
is P 2, one of London
Country's first coaches
specifically for
excursion/private
hire work (left).

AN 71 in Gossops Green on an ex-Southdown route. Southdown relinquished all its town routes to LC in April 1971 *(centre far left)*.

Usually single-deck, the 434 had AN 89 in use due to heavy Saturday demands on the Horsham-Crawley Down shorts *(centre left)*.

MBS 417 picks up in new Broadfield, the last estate of the original Crawley New Town plan *(lower left)*. Bewbush is a subsequent development. Route 478 is part of a system cross-linking Crawley's "villages" through the centre.

A graphic indication of Crawley's continuing growth is given by these maps of LT/LCBS operations in 1960 and 1977.

The 405 from West Croydon was still crew operated in July 1977. RCL 2219 (RG) looks menacing as it negotiates parked vehicles and lush trees in the bus station *(above)*.

MBSs on local routes vie with passengers in the High Street and the bus station *(below)*. Note the 478 'lazy' blind display.

London Country have established their central works at Tinsley Green, a facility much needed when the split from LT occurred.

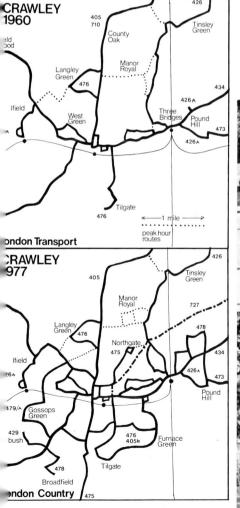

Where London's country ends another company's territory begins.

Enlightened thinking on the part of companies and local authorities has broken down the artificial boundaries found in some border towns where cross-town journeys could often be awkward.

Co-operation, and the transfer of services between companies where necessary, has made more economic use of resources and benefited the public by more closely relating the system to needs. Such a scheme was implemented at Gravesend in 1976 involving Maidstone & District.

Whether a route pattern has changed or whether it is as it always has been, London's green border towns provide a wealth of interest for enthusiast and student of transport alike.

Horsham has a 'natural' bus station with the layout of its Carfax, and planners should note how well its many functions work together. Always a frontier town between London Transport, Southdown and Aldershot & District with interest from a few independents, chiefly from the northern hinterland, later it became London Country and Alder Valley that met Southdown, but the pattern of routes remained similar.

LT operated the 434 to Crawley, East Grinstead and Edenbridge and the 414 to Dorking, Redhill and Croydon for many years, but in the 1950s double-deck 405 from Croydon via Crawley took over the 434 Crawley-Horsham road. However, the 434 (with its derivative, 473) regained its Horsham terminus from the 405 a decade later. The 414 meanwhile remained unchanged.

Side-engined Q 51 (CY) at the Carfax in 1951 on a 434 short working to Dormansland *(below)*.

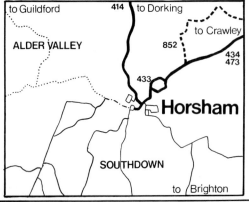

When the independent Hants & Sussex straggled empire crumbled, LT acquired their route from Horsham through Faygate and Lambs Green to Crawley. Numbered 852, this roundabout rural ride faded out in 1965. GS 54 (CY), at the same spot, has just arrived one Saturday morning in 1964 *(top right)*.

Horsham in recent years has redeveloped considerably, but the devastation of much of its character was necessary for survival at all in the face of rival attractions of nearby Crawley New Town. The Carfax and West Street keep their charm but new buildings aren't always in character with the old. Decide for yourself with this view of NBC-liveried RCL 2222 (RG) on the 414 *(below right)*.

The 'border' town of Sevenoaks was reached by East Surrey and Maidstone & District in 1914, and by Autocar in 1919. The bus station opened in 1936, was simply known as 'car park' for several years.

A petrol-engined M&D Leyland waits beside demoted 10T10 T 645 on the 413A in 1949 *(top)*. Started as a West Kent Motor Services route from Sevenoaks to Edenbridge via Ide Hill and Four Elms in 1928, it was cut back to Four Elms when LT acquired West Kent in 1939.

Their Heverham service, also of 1928, was replaced by Country Area 421 at the same time. T 427 (DG), a 9T9 variant still with its bumper, in 1949 *(middle left)*.

With radiator filler flap open, RF 612 (DG) leaves the bus station for Ide Hill in 1965 *(lower left)*. The 413A was completely withdrawn a year or so before London Country's formation, while the 421 was revised soon after *(see page 6)*.

Trunk 403, seen in 1965 with RT 4759 (CM) Tonbridge bound *(centre right)*, revised and renumbered 403A in 1972, was further renumbered 483 in 1973. SNC 162 in Green Line livery in a similar position in 1977 *(below right)*. Notice the change in vehicle direction in later years.

48

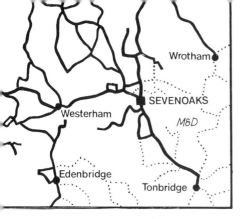

The 454 originated as a 1928 Autocar/Redcar route from Tonbridge to Sevenoaks via Weald. An early STL, with by then sagging bodywork, on the northern section to Chipstead tacked on in LT days *(above)*.

High Wycombe

Handcross

After Aylesbury, High Wycombe is the most westerly town served by London Country. RML 2412 is passing Alder Valley National 269, both on local services *(above)*. The Routemaster is on the 326, which serves Sands, the most westerly part of LC operations from the town. This route became s/d OMO on 1st October 1977, when HE closed.

Handcross, the most southerly point, four miles south of Crawley, was first served by East Surrey in 1922. This rural tentacle was regained when Southdown's 23A passed to London Country in 1971 *(see page 44)*. SMW 3 (CY), by the Red Lion in July 1977, on one of the few journeys to reach Handcross *(below)*, the regular terminus being the delightfully named village of Pease Pottage, closer to Crawley.

where red & green meet

There are many points on the inner edge of London's country where red and green meet and even overlap, Green Lines of course penetrating the entire diameter of the Central Area.

Motionless, two red RTs sandwich a DMS at Enfield while Green Line RP 82 sails on by *(above)*.

Enfield is within the GLC area, but St Albans certainly isn't. Behind front-entrance green STL 1491 in 1948, Central STL 313 pulls out to return from red isolation to the comfort of her red sisters in London's northern suburbs *(left)*. The inner terminus of 'out-on-a-limb' rural 84 route was later changed from Arnos Grove to New Barnet, making it even less 'Londonish'!

At Orpington Station in 1949, on the SE edge of London Transport's red domain, green Cub C 36 (DG) waits in front of a vintage-looking ST *(lower right)*. The 471 route is mentioned on page 56.

Thames-side Tale

Gravesend had a complex route network into its southern hinterland, mostly GS operated from NF. For several years the 489 ran to Ash and the 489A to Meopham, but a chain of developments in the early '70s altered the bus map in this corner considerably. Meopham lost all London buses in 1972 and Ash now was reached by a derivative of the Hartley Court 490, numbered 490A. The 489 number was resurrected for this in July 1973 and the 490 diverted away from Hartley Court to run to Ash also.

The first of the BNs, 24-30, were allocated to NF and ventured on to the 489 from September 1974. A June downpour in 1977 caught BN 27 at Gravesend on the new 489 *(above)*. 11 years before, GS 53 in High Street traffic on a garage journey of the old 489 *(lower)*.

Roadside Tale

Burford Street, Hoddesdon, seen elsewhere in this book, has been used by Country buses for many years, although more recent traffic schemes have repositioned the bus stop.

RF 554 (HG) stands beside the LT style stop flag in August 1976 *(above)*. In contrast, BN 49 (HG) was caught five months later beside the new style flag, one appearing throughout the country as a standard design for bus stops *(right)*.

Six months later still, more traffic schemes had erased all traces of this stop, a new one being provided closer to the town centre. For that matter the 327 had been 'erased' too, under timetable adjustments shortly after the photograph was taken.

A County Council supported experiment started in the Oxted area in November 1976, 'village bus' 465. It linked, certain days only, outlying areas that had lost their bus connection to Oxted in recent years and could be operated by the spare bus at CM, previously little-used but a necessary allocation. Chalkpit Wood and Biggin Hill were served three days a week, Tandridge on two days, and Crockham Hill just one day.

Emphasising the short ECW bodywork, a telephoto lens caught BN 52 dropping down into Crockham Hill on the Thursdays only morning run in that direction *(top left)*.

A few moments later she was loading up with a full complement of passengers *(lower left)*. The extremely competitive flat fare of 15p (child 8p) was an added attraction. Shoppers would have 1hr 40min in Oxted before returning on the midday bus.

Although officially bus RFs vanished from CM in 1974, the summer of 1977 saw RF 684, coincidentally a CM bus of ten years earlier, in use. On the Tuesday second Tandridge run she is seen at the foot of the hill in the village *(lower right)*.
A Postbus from Oxted to Lingfield was introduced in 1973, also serving Tandridge.

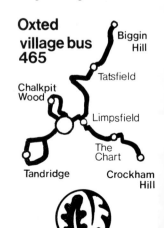

Oxted village bus 465

Biggin Hill
Tatsfield
Chalkpit Wood
Limpsfield
The Chart
Tandridge
Crockham Hill

In warm April sunshine RF 682 (DG) speeds through Brasted Chart on its return to Sevenoaks in 1966 *(top)*. The 413, running along the magnificent and very high, deeply wooded Greensand Ridge, with its breathtaking views across the Weald of Kent, was replaced in 1972 by a 404 extension to Ide Hill only, shown by RF 201 (DG) in weather less clement *(lower)*.

This location is also in **a London RF album**, where buses on the 413A, serving Four Elms at the foot of the hill, were featured. It was West Kent territory in earlier times. *(see page 48).*

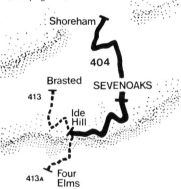

the North Downs

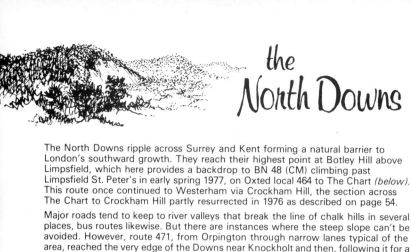

The North Downs ripple across Surrey and Kent forming a natural barrier to London's southward growth. They reach their highest point at Botley Hill above Limpsfield, which here provides a backdrop to BN 48 (CM) climbing past Limpsfield St. Peter's in early spring 1977, on Oxted local 464 to The Chart *(below)*. This route once continued to Westerham via Crockham Hill, the section across The Chart to Crockham Hill partly resurrected in 1976 as described on page 54.

Major roads tend to keep to river valleys that break the line of chalk hills in several places, bus routes likewise. But there are instances where the steep slope can't be avoided. However, route 471, from Orpington through narrow lanes typical of the area, reached the very edge of the Downs near Knockholt and then, following it for a few miles, turned back towards Orpington again. At Scotts Lodge, a matter of yards from the very crest and where the route turned 'inland' again, GS 10 (DG) evokes Country bus memories typical of the fifties and early sixties *(right)*.

The Mole gap between Dorking and Leatherhead separates Ranmore from its more famous neighbour, Boxhill. Route 433, which also served Leith Hill on the Greensand Ridge *(see page 36)*, for many years served this popular common high on the Downs, where C 77 (DS) was seen in 1951 *(lower right)*. Dorking local 412 replaced the 433 over this section in 1968, joined by summer Sundays only 417 'Rambler's Bus' in 1977.

The Green Line system developed in the early thirties as a network of limited-stop semi-luxury services for fast travel to Town from London's country centres. A useful cross-linking of routes was a logical development and by the close of the pre-war decade a well publicised, well patronised system was in operation. Green Line was a household word and the prestige that had become attached to it an enviable and valuable quality. Whereas ordinary travellers went by bus, Green Line passengers would 'take the coach'.

Undoubtedly snob appeal and the sense of exclusiveness was a certain attraction in the days before widespread car ownership, and maybe this was also a contributory factor to the falling from favour experienced by the Green Line system from the early sixties onwards. As coach travel generally adapted to modern needs and upped its standards to mean fast, competitive and convenient travel, so the questionable luxury of an extra inch of padding to a bus seat and a conductor to collect your fares in what was otherwise an elderly bus, became an anachronism. Passengers were no longer enamoured by the thought of Green Line travel. The glamour had faded, the prestige was lost — it was just another bus service by and large.

Inevitable and sensible one-man-operation spread through the Green Line system towards the end of the sixties. Various experiments were tried to effect a better system, some successful, some not so. Unreliability of new RPs (delivered in 1971) didn't help and despite their coach style seats they were still externally a bus. Arrival of Leyland Nationals from 1972, at first with bus seats, was an insult to the once highly esteemed service. RFs still soldiered on but their age did little good for the tarnished Green Line image.

London Country had two choices — to let the system die a slow and undignified death with all the inherent bad publicity that would result, or give it a boost — make it viable once more, relate it to present day needs. There was still a scraping of goodwill on which a modern useful system could be made to work.

GREEN LINE

Curtailments and reductions in the '60s and early '70s were an economic necessity. The 706 was a 1977 casualty, well-covered by other services for most of its length. However, in compensation the 708 was extended to Aylesbury and the successful summer extensions of the 706 to Chartwell, former home of Winston Churchill, below Westerham, replaced by a double-running diversion to some 705 (Sevenoaks-Windsor) journeys in both directions. SNC 140 (DG), formerly a CM 706 vehicle, takes a full complement of passengers through Hosey Hill to the revered statesman's splendid home *(top right)*.

One of the biggest Green Line successes stems from LT days, from 1967 and introduction of the 727 linking Crawley & Gatwick Airport to Heathrow, Watford Junction, Luton and later Luton Airport. It achieved an amazing number of connections at strategic points and consistently high loadings have been an ever present feature, especially between Heathrow and Crawley. The original daily hourly frequency was increased to half-hourly for the summer season over this section in May 1977. New RS 7 (SA) pulls away from Watford Junction towards Luton just a week before the improved timetable started *(lower right)*. Special luggage racks fitted behind the driver's position can be seen.

Individual timetable/faretable leaflets have always been part of Green Line publicity. The 727 route diagram emphasises the wealth of other transport connections *(below)*.

Thus the hope of the new Green Line system lay in opening up new facilities rather than duplicating already well-served ones. To this end great emphasis was put on, for example, facilities to Heathrow from Town and from out of Town centres, promoted as 'The Airport Connection' *(opposite)*. This was a joint promotion with Alder Valley, whose Reading-London express services also linked in at Heathrow.

The other radical improvement for the Green Lines was, at long last, real coaches — new AEC Reliances with either Duple Dominant (RB Reliance/Blackpool) or Plaxton Panorama Supreme (RS Reliance/Scarborough) full-luxury specification coach bodies in an individual and distinctive version of the familiar National white coach livery. The experimental RC class of 1965 *(see page 72)* was first finished in a similar and quite striking livery of pale grey with a green band but soon adopted the drab, by comparison, Lincoln green with a pale green band.

The striking but rather jazzy front end styling of Duple Dominant RB 21, leaning heavily with the camber, gets admiring glances from intending passengers in Hoddesdon. Its deep windscreen has a tinted top section to reduce glare, a problem with such designs. This 715 will end up at Guildford, but the intermediate points cannot be easily displayed on the narrow blind aperture *(above)*.

GREEN LINE ALDER VALLEY

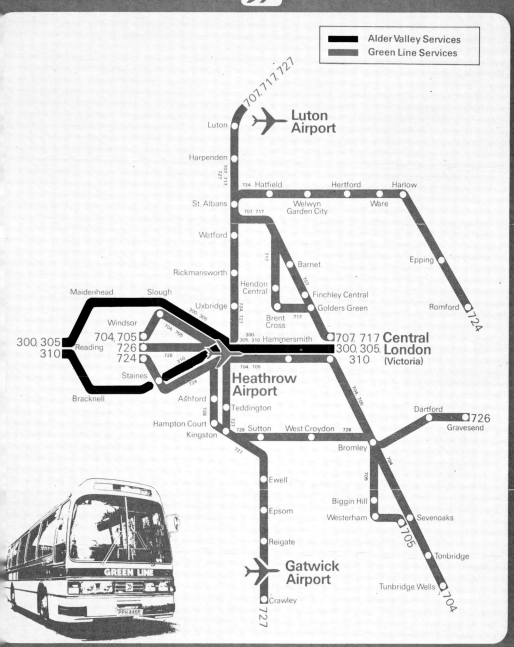

Legend:
- Alder Valley Services
- Green Line Services

Luton Airport — 707, 717, 727
Luton
Harpenden — 707, 717, 727
Hatfield — 724
Hertford
Harlow
St. Albans — 707, 717
Welwyn Garden City
Ware
Watford
Barnet — 717
Epping
Rickmansworth
Hendon Central
Finchley Central — 707
Golders Green
Romford — 724
Maidenhead
Slough
Uxbridge — 300, 305
Brent Cross — 717
704, 705
Windsor
704, 705
Reading — 726
724 727
Hammersmith — 300, 305, 310
707, 717 Central London 300, 305 310 (Victoria)
300, 305 310
726
Staines — 310
704, 705
Bracknell
Heathrow Airport
Ashford
Teddington
726
Dartford
726 Gravesend
Hampton Court
727
Kingston — 726 Sutton
West Croydon — 726
704 705
Bromley
704
Ewell
705
Biggin Hill
Epsom
Westerham
Sevenoaks
705
Reigate
Tonbridge
Gatwick Airport
Tunbridge Wells — 704
Crawley — 727

The Airport Network

A regular, daily network of express services linking Heathrow Airport with Central London, Gatwick Airport, Luton Airport and major towns over a large area, provided by Green Line & Alder Valley.

Full details are available in a leaflet from enquiry offices, airport information desks or by post from:
London Country, Bell Street, Reigate, Surrey RH2 7LE. Tel : Reigate 42411.

Green Lines haven't always had a 'green line'. In pre-war days the lighter relief colour was generally applied to the window area of the body and this style particularly suited coaches of the day.

In marked contrast to RF times — RFs diligently performed Green Line duties for about 20 years continuously (some longer) — pre-war policy was for coaches to be demoted to bus work after a few years service. The 7T7 versions of T-class AEC Regals, delivered in two batches in 1930 & 31, were ousted as early as 1938 when singularly handsome 10T10s arrived. The 9T9 version of 1936, similar to subsequent 10T10s but with bonnet and wings faired into the bodywork, replaced a motley collection acquired from independents.

Preserved T 219, a later 7T7, at the 1964 HCVC Brighton run with 'period' driver standing by *(below)*.

These Ts weren't the only pre-war coaches. London Transport was the largest operator of AEC's famous side-engined Q with 233 single-deckers & 5 double-deckers in stock. 50 of the single-deckers were Green Lines delivered towards the end of 1936, their duties being on the Hertford-Byfleet/Guildford M1/M2/M3 from HG & GF, the H3 Luton-London from LS, and also routes Q & R from High Wycombe to London (MA & HE). Some were also at WY. These 6Q6 versions had 32-seat centre-entrance Park Royal bodywork with an obvious 'London' look.

The revolutionary Leyland-built TF class was an early essay in underfloor-engined chassis arrangement. The 1937 prototype was followed by 12 private hire examples, all but one destroyed by enemy action during the war, and then 75 regular coaches in 1939. With LPTB bodies, again possessing an obvious family resemblance, they saw little service before war broke out but on reinstatement of Green Line routes from 1946 their main home was Dorking routes 712/3/4 and Aldgate routes 720/23.

TF 77 (GY) on the 723 passes STL 1521 (GY) in Grays on the first day of 1952 *(top left)*. The bus is working the 37A between Grays and Tilbury via Chadwell St Mary, one of several local routes taken over from Eastern National the previous September. The following day it merged with the 370 to become Romford-Tilbury.

Later in the same month TFs at Grays were ousted by new Green Line RFs, the displaced TFs taking up bus duties elsewhere. Several went to SA and received bus livery accordingly. June 1952 saw TF 6? (LS) reliving past glories working the 714 to Luton and, although in bus livery, carrying side destination boards *(top right)*. RFs had been allocated to the 714 three months earlier.

WELWYN

HATFIELD

POTTERS
BAR

717

LONDON
MARBLE
ARCH

RICHMOND

KINGSTON

WEYBRIDGE

WOKING   1. 5. 46.

A feature of post-war operation was the replacement of pre-war route letters by numbers in the 700 range, similarly arranged — i.e. in an anti-clockwise pattern starting from Gravesend. The opposite tentacles were permutated slightly differently, with some sections abandoned and some new roads opened up.

The 717 was introduced on 1st May 1946 from Woking to Welwyn Garden City, operated by 10T10s from WY & HF. T 484 (HF) Woking-bound in February 1952, a matter of days before RFs took over *(lower right)*. In October 1955 this route was renumbered 716A and diverted from Welwyn to Stevenage, a new 717 being introduced from Victoria to Welwyn (withdrawn 1967).

An interesting comparison can be made between the Park Royal Green Line Qs and the BRCW Country bus Qs at Eccleston Bridge, Victoria, on the 6th June 1949. Heavy loadings and relief journeys were a common feature of those difficult years.

The 712/3 from Dorking to Luton/Dunstable, mentioned previously as being TF operated, had Qs in charge on that day. Q 213 (SA) well-loaded on a relief to St. Albans *(top left)*. The engine position is easily visible on southbound Q 222 (DS), also with a full complement of passengers *(top right)*. Note the unusual combined head/sidelamp arrangement.

Bus Q 80 (SA) waits to take a relief 712 away from Eccleston Bridge *(lower left)*. This location, after the closure of Poland Street Coach Station in 1933, became the main London boarding point for Green Lines. Q 55 (EG), another BRCW-bodied bus, offloading on a 708 relief to East Grinstead *(lower right)*.

In May 1966, the same location as on the page before had RF 217 (ST) Gravesend bound *(above)*. She and her sister coaches were due for a skilful facelift shortly afterwards that enabled the class to continue in service for virtually another decade. No number was carried on the side roof boards for this route since the 701/2, like the 706/7, were interworked, hence 'ASCOT or SUNNINGDALE'. Roof board practice faded out at the end of the '60s, a Green Line trademark from the beginning. Ten years later both 701 and 702 had faded out, too.

Green Line

'SIXTIES SCENES

Introduction of Routemaster coaches when accompanied by a timetable reduction was sometimes a false economy, since the public couldn't reconcile extra seats with wider headways, and consequently traffic was lost. The 708 got RMCs at the end of 1967, and frequency was reduced from half-hourly to hourly. By 1969 loadings had fallen so that RFs could be reintroduced on a one-for-one basis. RMC 1516 (EG) reflects the early morning sun on a fine June day at Godstone in 1968 *(below)*.

Actually a '70s scene but a similar situation could be found in the late '60s. The new face as applied to RF 183 at Victoria working the 718 to Windsor *(right)*.

An LT bulls-eye transfer was positioned between the headlights at first, replaced by the London Country 'flying polo' in the early '70s. Later the space was left blank. Had RFs been destined for longer Green Line service (!) the National 'N' would have no doubt appeared in that space.

RMC 4 (EP) with original front at Harlow in 1963, a few weeks before the new Harlow (HA) garage opened, replacing Epping *(left upper)*, and after modification Wrotham bound at Victoria on the 717 *(left upper)*.

The 717 Welwyn-Victoria *(see page 65)* had been extended to Wrotham in November 1964 to replace the former 703. The 717 was later curtailed at Baker Street, and later still replaced by a 719 extension.

RMC 4, as the other Routemaster coaches, took on bus duties at the end of the decade *(see page 13)* and in 1976 was further modified by the fitting of quarter-drop opening windows to the front upper deck.

Southern peripheral 725 from Gravesend to Windsor avoiding London was introduced in 1953, a success from the word go. It wasn't until May 1977 that a logical diversion to serve Heathrow occurred. Alternate journeys were diverted via Heathrow and the M4, numbered 726, while the others continued via Staines as 725. SMA 19, eastbound in Bromley on the new 726 *(above)*. Compare its NBC Green Line livery with that of SMA 20 on page 25. The 726 acquired new RBs the following autumn.

In January 1977 the 712/3 and northern half of 714 were revised and replaced by two new routes, 707/17, providing a basic hourly service between Victoria and Luton Airport, alternate journeys (717) via the new Brent Cross shopping complex and Borehamwood. Scheduled for operation by new RS coaches, when RP 12 (SA) made an unscheduled appearance at Brent Cross on the 707, a paper sticker had to be used as there were no appropriate blinds to fit the RP aperture *(below)*. The 707 and 717 numbers had been used in previous years for completely different routes.

Green Line
Ts demoted

All 9T9 & 10T10 coaches were converted to public ambulances at the start of the war, but several of the latter were reconverted for passenger use soon afterwards and put to bus work for the duration.

T 429, a 9T9, regained passenger service in August 1945 and like her sisters took on bus duties (some painted red for the Central Area). In 1949 she was seen disgorging passengers in Epsom suburbs (above).

T 446 (NF) in more rural Kent the same year (right). The integral nature of the bonnet and wings can be seen in these views.

The 10T10s returned to Green Line work from 1946 until ousted by new RFs in 1951/2. Many saw further brief service as buses, 40 'reddened' for Central work. T 614 (EP) in green bus livery at Hertford, heading for the northern outpost of Country operation at Letchworth (lower right). The externally-sliding door can be compared with the internal arrangement of the Weymann-built 9T9s.

RC
1965-1977

RC1 entering Westerham shortly after in†
livery *(centre)*, and as a nocturnal bus at
Green Line livery *(right)*.

Amid a blaze of publicity the fourteen RC
class AEC Reliances entered Green Line
service in 1965, initially on the 705 from
DG and WR. Coupled with air
suspension, their sleek, cleanly-styled 36'
BET Federation 'express' bodies with 8'
window bays, forced ventilation and
coach seats, were intended to bring new
standards of comfort to Green Line travel
(and, presumably, new passengers too!).

At first in a striking pale grey with broad
green band, they were later repainted
into standard two-tone green, drab by
comparison. They then worked other
Green Line routes, including the 727
(fitted inside with extra luggage racks,
later removed from most) and the 723.
Regrettably, reliability failed to match
comfort and, despite mechanical
modifications, the class was relegated to
bus duties at Hertford in 1974.

RC 7 (RG) in Epsom while on the 727
(below).

RC 4 (HG) on bus work but still in Green
Line colours *(below)*.

They were withdrawn in January 1977,
rendered redundant by timetable
changes, but four were kept for training
purposes. RC 11 had been destroyed by
fire in 1971.

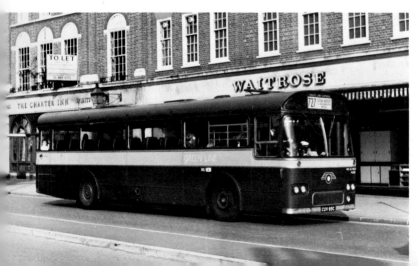

RC 10 & 13 in bus
1976. The sleek Wi
lines are emphasi
side view *(right &)*

n in its imaginative first
975 in hybrid NBC bus/

K

e).

301
sixties &
seventies

Aylesbury
Tring
Hemel Hempstead
Watford

The Bassom numbering system of the 1924 London Traffic Act resulted in those National routes entering the Metropolitan area assuming numbers between 301 and 350 (similarly with East Surrey between 401 and 450). Though LT abandoned this system, nevertheless northern Country routes took the 3XX range and southern 4XX, until the 8XX range was introduced for new routes.

National's Watford-Aylesbury route became 301 and thus in a sense was the premier Country route. Aylesbury, incidentally, was well outside the LPTB area.

Roof-box RT 607 (TG) on a garage journey in 1962 *(above)*. Hemel Hempstead's growth benefited the 301. Leaving the town in 1977, LNB 25 (HH) (ex-LNC) was bound for the inner terminus of Little Bushey beyond Watford *(below)*. The Merlin behind is working town route H1, part of a system implemented in January 1977 following the similar scheme in St Albans *(see page 38)*.

West
Croydon

Godstone

404

Lingfield

S 22
24

East
Grinstead

Hartfield

Forest
Row

24

Chelwood
Gate

Uckfield

The 409's origins lie in a 1916 route by East Surrey from Reigate to Hartfield via Godstone and East Grinstead, replaced by S9 from West Croydon to either Hartfield or Chelwood Gate in June 1922. That October the Chelwood Gate leg was extended to Uckfield giving a route length of some 32 miles. Uckfield remains the most far flung point ever reached by any 'Country Area' route.

79 in the East Surrey fleet, an ex-WD AEC YC fitted in 1922 with a secondhand body from a B-type, had been in service a year when photographed with 'period' crew at Uckfield (top). An extension to the S22 from Reigate (later only Horley) replaced the Hartfield section in 1924, itself replaced in June 1926 by a 404 extension, reverting to S22 operation that October. The S22 was then replaced entirely by new route 24, joint with Autocar, to Tunbridge Wells (see map).

141, a Ransomes 48-seat bodied AEC PS of 1924, en route from Uckfield, by then renumbered 409 to conform with Metropolitan Police regulations (lower). The advance in bus design in the twenties is evident but the fussier fleetname?

Being outside the LPTB area Uckfield lost its 'London' service in 1933, but LT had running powers beyond the designated area to continue serving Forest Row. In the past green Rover tickets were invalid beyond East Grinstead because of this.

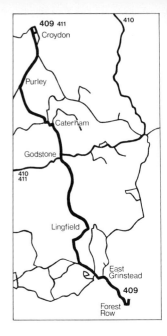

southern trunk 409

over the years

Front-entrance STL 1466 (GD) at Purley in 1947 *(top left)*. Its wartime restricted blind display contrasts with the wealth of information on RT 1047 (GD) at Godstone garage in 1965 *(middle far left)*.

The 409/410/411 were the first Country routes to get Routemasters, on 3rd October 1965. Delays in green RML delivery caused a temporary influx of new red RMLs, like 2300 (GD) at Newchapel on the second day of Routemaster operation *(middle left)*. At Godstone garage the same day red RML 2287 leads 2306, the first of the green examples *(lower left)*. While in the Country Area these red RMLs carried notices that green Rover tickets were usable on them.

In the first London Country livery, RML 2312 (GD) in East Grinstead *(above)*. At Newchapel again, heading the other way from 2300 opposite, is 2333 (GD) in full NBC colours in 1974 *(below)*.

non standard 410

Route 410 will always be remembered for its low height buses, necessitated until 1964 by a low bridge in Oxted, one that gave the distinct impression that even these low buses wouldn't squeeze under, especially at speed!

Up to 1934 open-top buses had been the 410 norm but in April that year 12 unique lowbridge AEC Regents were placed in service between Reigate and Bromley by the LPTB, ordered as one of the last autonomous acts by London General Country Services whose livery they initially wore. These 'Godstone STLs', as they were called, were totally non-standard among the class and were unique to the 410 for nearly 20 years.

The elegant lines of their handsome front entrance Weymann bodies (with the added distinction of a sliding door!) can be seen on STL 1044 (GD) at Godstone Green *(left),* and STL 1048 (GD) in post-war livery filling up at Bromley *(below).*

RLH 37 (GD), well loaded in 1963, passes through Biggin Hill, famous for its airfield important in World War Two *(above)*.

Non-standard RLHs, mentioned on page 30, worked the 410 from 1950 to November 1964 when LT, in order to make operation at GD more efficient, integrated 410 schedules with the 409/411 and replaced RLHs with RTs. This meant a long circuitous and unpopular diversion in Oxted to avoid the offending low bridge in Bluehouse Lane. Local protest pressed the Council to lower the road under the bridge and from 15th May 1966 the 410 resumed its original route, by now RML operated.

RT 3050 (GD) in Oxted, facing Bromley direction but bound for Reigate due to the complicated diversion *(middle right)*.

RML 2317 (GD) passes under the bridge that caused all the trouble over the years. The sign still indicates only 14' headroom! *(lower right)*

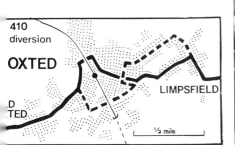

410 diversion

OXTED

LIMPSFIELD

D TED

½ mile

RML 2310 (GD) by the school on Limpsfield Common in 1966 *(above)*. Six years later route 410 scored another first when GD, the first garage to get Country RMLs, received new AF Fleetlines in February 1972 *(see page 18)*. These brought a new livery to London Country — paler green than before, relieved by a large area of Canary yellow around the lower deck windows — and marked the start of widespread double-deck OMO. Leaflets were distributed locally, informing the public of the changes *(left)*.

Nearly 50 years before! The notorious Oxted bridge kept open-top PS ('provincial' S) types on the 410 when covered-top buses had taken over elsewhere in East Surrey's territory. Thirty were delivered in 1924, the property of LGOC, but twelve actually sold to East Surrey soon afterwards. No. 130 remained a General vehicle but was kept for the 410 *(below)*.

When changes were made to Hertford area routes in early 1977 a new number entered the scheme. New 316 directly replaced the 310A between Enfield and Hoddesdon, Rye House, and continued to Hertford via St Margarets and Ware, directly replacing the 327 north of Broxbourne. The Broxbourne-Nazeing section was replaced by a 392 diversion. Always busy routes with a narrow headway, the 310A variation also once served Ponders End between Enfield and Cheshunt.

orthern trunk
310
Hoddesdon

Hoddesdon Clock
ower and RT 986 (HG)
above). It still carried
wartime restricted blind
isplay in 1951.

ome 25 years later, an
T still in charge. 3520
HG) in one-way
urford Street (right).

Worm's-eye view of
N 119 (HG) in sunny
igh Street on the new
16 Enfield-bound
ower right).

Ware
310
ertford
310A
Hoddesdon
oxbourne
Cheshunt
310
310A
field

1976

5 miles

Red buses have frequently strayed on to green routes in the past. An increase in requirements, temporary absence of vehicles for overhaul, or shortage for other reasons has often brought Town buses to Country roads. Strangely, the reverse has been less common, though Kingston has at odd times seen Country single-deckers on its, almost country, red routes.

Red on green was particularly common in the early post-war period when LT, like many operators, faced great difficulties in meeting demands. A confusing picture was thus presented to the travelling public.

Further confusion could have resulted from the unfamiliar entrance position on red STL 1793, caught in April 1947 on a short working of green route 414 (left). Towards the end of the war she acquired her central entrance/exit with sliding door, and was used for pay-as-you-board experiments at Kingston, the conductor being seated behind a cash desk just inside the entrance. When sent to the Country Area normal fare collection was used.

Of course, a number of buses were permanently transferred to the Country Area and received green livery accordingly, a handful of rear-engined CR types being such a case (see page 20). CR 4 (EP), however, had red livery when on green route 393 (below). What about that petrol pump!

red buses on green

During the severe vehicle shortages of the early '70s, a large number of red Merlins were on loan to London Country and could be found operating from many garages. MB 136, one of the low driving position buses unpopular with LT, at the head of a long line of assorted types at Watford (right lower).

Rare for red RTLs, Leyland versions of the RT, to work green routes, it was even rarer for any red buses to work Green Line routes. However, in 1964 red RTL 911 (GM) was caught at Egham on Green Line 718 *(left)*.

The comparison trials between XF and XA types brought red buses of an identical appearance in place of green on the 424 temporarily *(see page 16)*. XA 38 (EG) at the Imberhorne Estate terminus at East Grinstead in 1966 *(middle)*.

To meet operating demands London Country had to hire vehicles from wherever they could. Throughout 1975/6/7 particularly, a rainbow of hired buses could be seen alongside familiar green ones.

Dunton Green had Royal Blue coaches in National white, like 1423, a later Bristol MW/ECW, near Sevenoaks Bat and Ball on the 404 to Shoreham *(top)*.

Inside Chelsham garage is blue and cream Maidstone Borough Council 35, an Atlantean/ Massey *(middle left)*. The 453, between Warlingham and Caterham-on-the-Hill, was a new route started by London Transport in 1934.

all sorts on green

Also blue and cream is 345, an attractive Southend PD3/East Lancs, working from Harlow in October 1976 *(middle right)*. This was one of several previously on hire to London Transport.

Bournemouth hired both single and double-deck deep primrose Daimlers to London Country, the single-deckers being Roadliners. At Dorking, however, is their Fleetline/MCW 194 on the 470 *(lower)*. The 470 is mentioned on page 36. It was curtailed at West Croydon from 1972.

SNAP!

AN 85 and RP 41 demonstrate the interchangeable front body panels and windscreens of their Park Royal bodies. Notice the twin headlights and air intake of the Reliance.

outside Inns

SNC 182 (RG) on the double run to serve Gerrards Cross Station by The Packhorse, when the 711 still ran.

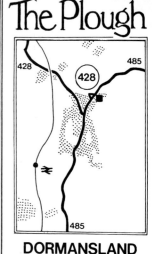

Dormansland Plough was the haunt of RFs during the '50s and much of the '60s, and is shown in **a London RF album** with these vehicles coming and going.

Recasting of services through this Surrey corner in 1975 — both Kent and Sussex are within a mile or two — meant the 434 had shrunk to operate from Horsham to East Grinstead, with only a few weekday peak 473s and infrequent Sunday 434s still reaching Dormansland. The Westerham to Edenbridge 485 was projected on to East Grinstead through Dormansland on a similar hourly headway as replacement.

The 428 remained unaffected by these changes and NBC-liveried XA 1 (EG) has just arrived at The Plough on a crisp March morning in 1976 *(above)*.

Double-deckers have also appeared on some school workings to Dormansland of the 409. In recent years this location has seen Swifts, Merlins and Nationals pass through and terminate, wearing a variety of liveries as the LT/NBC changeover took effect. In National colours, 2-door Merlin MBS 295 (CY) in November of the same year waits at The Plough. It is Horsham bound on a Sunday 434 with not a passenger in sight *(below)*.

The Old House at Home in Edenbridge has seen many changes to the area's bus routes over the years. Events outlined on the previous page have banished the long-established 434 from Kent, leaving the extended 485 alone to meet Maidstone & District operations along the road by this Inn. In summer sun RF 634 (CY) passes the tile-hung facade of the then Fremlins house in 1966 *(below)*.

The 485 also passes Crockham Hill's Royal Oak, midway between Westerham and Edenbridge. It is just one of the dozen pubs SNC 200 (EG) will pass en route *(above)*, including The Old House at Home and The Plough.

Kentish Inns

green buses and

Trees and scaffolding, a seat, shoppers and traffic — Horsham Carfax in 1974 with RCL 2259 (RG), demoted from its original Green Line work, on the 414 to Croydon via Dorking and Reigate *(left)*. Note the London Country logo.

When the 410 still ran on Sundays! RML 2317 (GD) comes up by Limpsfield Church in 1966 past churchgoers' parked cars under enormous lime trees. The bus is on its temporary circuitous diversion avoiding the then low bridge in Oxted *(right)*.
(See page 79.)

trees

Trees are an attractive part of the Country Bus scene. Their lush foliage in summer, gilded autumn tones or bare winter branches present an ever changing background to many a bus route in London's country.

Summer evening at Pound Hill with long shadows and spreading trees. RT 3391 (CY) with top-deck front windows wide open on flyover from town route 426A (top).

Starling's-eye view of RT 4548 (RG) climbing Reigate Hill in 1967 (lower).

East Surrey, sometimes with the help of the LGOC if within the Metropolitan area, pioneered the provision of largish garages in its area and consequently most of the southern Country Area garages were built before London Transport took control in 1933.

Green Line SNC 71 (EG), displaying blinds for local 435, enjoys having its nose in the June sunshine 49 years after East Grinstead garage was opened *(above)*. That was on 1st August 1925, replacing stabling facilities at The Crown used since 1922. The final site in Garland Road was the third to be considered, others being unsatisfactory for several reasons. The premises were enlarged in 1927.

A combination of misty evening sunshine and a poor camera lend a period atmosphere to an early post-war line up at Chelsham *(below)*. The Cub on the left is for the 464 group, the 10T10s for the 706/7, while the STLs are for the 403/8/70 routes.

Chelsham was built at the same time as nearby Godstone and both opened the same day, 20th January 1925, replacing a number of outstations in the area, often at the back of local inns. Chelsham supplied buses for the 403 & 404. This latter route linked Croydon with East Grinstead via Chelsham, Oxted & Edenbridge. Chelsham too was enlarged, increasing its capacity in 1931 from 8 to 24 vehicles.

Amersham & District's buses that worked in the High Wycombe area in the late '20s were kept at Thames Valley's Wycombe Marsh garage until 1929, when High Wycombe garage opened (enlarged by LT later). Originally bearing the logical code of HW, this was soon changed to HE to avoid confusion with Central Area's Hanwell, also HW. Green Lines bearing High Wycombe's HW used to pass right by Hanwell.

Towards the end of 1947 Green Line 724 High Wycombe-London was linked to the 711 Reigate-London to form a new through 711 High Wycombe-Reigate. This was often the scene for experimental vehicles due to its range of operating conditions. Leyland Nationals were introduced in 1973 and in this view of High Wycombe garage SNC 183 rests beside SNC 185 (RG), about to leave for Reigate *(above)*.

The 711 was withdrawn in October 1977, replaced by new 790 from High Wycombe to Victoria on a two-hourly headway, interworked with Oxford/S Midland 290 (from Oxford) between these points. HE closed at the same time, its operations transferred to neighbouring MA. Note the National 'N' inside the previous LCBS logo shape on the wall.

A stranger in the camp! RF 312 (CM), one of the RFs with an unusual history of roles described in **a London RF album**, in 1965 nonchalantly basks in the sun half-inside Maidstone & District's Edenbridge depot, built 10 years earlier and used as a turning point and layover for country buses for many years *(lower right)*.

COUNTRY BUSES AT HOME

Crash!

Bus drivers are among the safest on the road, but accidents can still happen. On a 410 in early 1965, RT 3131 (GD) overturned at Keston on its way to Bromley, having first skidded 35 yards, knocking down a lamp post and bus stop into the bargain! No one was seriously injured but another 30' would have presented a stickier problem. The bus is seen here upright, after being expertly attended by LT's able rescue crew. Had the mishap occurred a year later it would have been a brand new Routemaster in the same sorry state.

Admiring glances for Bill Cottrell's preserved Q 83 at the 1974 Weymouth bus rally *(above)*. Southern National 262 alongside is newer, but the Q certainly is the younger looking one! Many former London buses have been preserved by many people, from London Transport down. There are examples of several types that once saw service in London's country and can now be seen at rallies up and down the country.

ever green

Of course, a lot of ex-Country buses have seen further regular revenue-earning service with other concerns or in use as contract vehicles or school buses.

A lot of books have been published about London's buses and, although green buses may have featured less than red, there is still a wealth of information, verbal and visual, available to the enthusiast and student. A full list would be too lengthy to include here, but for up-to-date information membership of the **London Omnibus Traction Society** is advised *(details overleaf)*. Their quarterly **London Bus Magazine** (available to non-members, too) is of first rate quality and contains articles of great interest, both topical and historical. They produce a wealth of useful and informative publications, of which the yearly **London Bus Review** is particularly recommended. **Capital Transport** publish an excellent **London Country Buses and Green Line Coaches** illustrated fleetlist book, among other London bus items. Ian Allan's **abc London Buses** has been published for many years, updated periodically. They also have published John Gray's **London Buses in Camera** and **London's Surburban Buses**. The Oakwood Press have produced various London bus books, including **The London Country Bus.**

However, better than our **London Country Bus album,** a living London Country Bus is a journey of exploration on the buses and routes that serve London's green. Without the public to travel on them, and that includes **you,** there would be no London Country Bus! — OK.

ever thankful!

It might have been possible to compile a book such as this using the photographs of just one individual. It might have been, but it wasn't. So we must thank the following people for allowing us to use their dedicated work in our London Country Bus album.

Thank you, then

J. H. Aston	**20**	CR 13, 33	Eamonn Kentell	**24**	SMW 11
	82	CR 4		**39**	BL 16
Alan B. Cross	**28**	C 60		**55**	RF 201
	32	STL 2562		**70**	SMA 19
	35	STL 2670		**83**	MB 136
	36	C 3	Lens of Sutton	**30**	RLH 43
	38	STL 2069		**33**	PTE 592, NLP 635, RW 1
	39	Q 87			
	40	STL 2693, RT 971, TF 7	L. A. Mack	**34**	RF 521
	41	C 31	Gerald Mead	**8**	RT 4509, 605
	48	T 645, 427		**28**	GS 42
	49	STL		**41**	GS 27
	51	STL 1491/313, C 36		**68**	RF 217
	57	C 77		**69**	RMC 4
	64	TF 77/STL 1521		**72**	RC 7
	65	TF 63, T 484		**83**	RTL 911
	66	Q 213, 80			
	67	Q 222, 55	Pamlin Prints	**34**	Q 47
	71	T 429, 446, 614		**35**	STL 1055
	74	RT 607		**75**	79, 141
	81	RT 986			
			Phil Picken	**41**	RF 604
J. Higham	**80**	130	Peter J. Relf	**79**	RLH 37
V. C. Jones	**34**	Q 26	Colin Stannard	**9**	RT 604
	36	TF 44		**18**	BT 6
	46	Q 51		**25**	SMA 20
	76	STL 1466, RML 2300, 2287/2306		**26**	LN 15
	78	STL 1048, 1044		**29**	GS 55, BL 19, BN 36
	82	STL 1793		**84**	1423, 345

Pages are indicated in bold type.

The copyright on all other pictures belongs to Viewfinder, and they have been drawn from the ever expanding Viewfinder collection, which includes the work of the two authors of this book, Ray Stenning and Trevor Whelan.

As Viewfinder wishes to be truly 'the bus scene seen', the publisher would like to hear from anyone who thinks they may have some topic or perhaps a collection of photographs that could help to achieve this aim. So do please drop us a line if you feel your 'thing' could be of use, but even if it is only to help illustrate one of the many books planned it will broaden our scope. We have been approached with various ideas already — some to be used definitely, some to be considered for future use, some beyond our possibilities. Into which category will yours fit?

PS, don't forget an SAE.

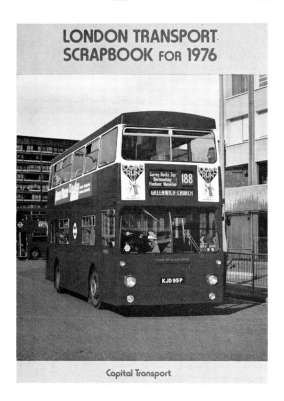

THERE'S LOTS MORE TO FIND OUT ABOUT LONDON'S BUSES

. . . through LOTS—the London Omnibus Traction Society.

What do you get for a £4.00 annual subscription? LOTS. A monthly news-letter with pictorial cover and full picture page, with all the news on London Transport and London Country. A monthly meeting in the centre of London. The chance to buy the quarterly "London Bus Magazine" at specially reduced rates. An information service to answer members' queries. And a well-stocked sales department.

There's LOTS for Londoners in LOTS. Send foolscap s.a.e. for sample newsletter and membership application to: Leslie Brush, 77 Boscombe Road, Worcester Park, Surrey KT4 8PJ.

THE LONDON OMNIBUS TRACTION SOCIETY

---

the London RF . . .

a loving visual tribute to London's famous RF buses & coaches as seen by two dedicated enthusiasts

a delightful study in pictures & words

sentimental & objective

companion to this volume

a London RF album

one of the expanding range of books from

 the bus scene seen!

ISBN 0 906051 00 2   £1.25 (+ 15p P&P if by post)